The Howard Morgen Fingerstyle Jc

The Ellington Collection
for
Solo Guitar

EDITOR: Aaron Stang

COVER DESIGN: Richard Chimelis / The Point

PHOTOGRAPHY: Gary Morgen Photography, Danbury, CT

1946 Epiphone Triumph courtesy of Joe Pichkur, The Guitar Center, Elmont, N.Y.
1929 Cadillac Convertible Coupe courtesy of George Ray, Middlebury, Connecticut

---

A companion cassette for this publication has been prepared by the author. The cassette features all of the book's solos as they appear in the text. This cassette is a valuable tool; not only as an aid in mastering these arrangements, but for making them "come alive" as entertaining pieces. To order (please specify "The Ellington Collection") send $9.95, plus $1.50 shipping and handling (N.Y. residents please add sales tax) to:

 GRACE COURT WEST PRODUCTIONS
P.O. Box 345, Great Neck, NY 11022

Contents

Foreword

Two of the songs included in this collection appear in my book "Concepts" and one is from "Fingerstyle Favorites." All three have been modified slightly and tablature has been included. The remaining nine selections originally appeared in segmented form in my fingerstyle jazz column in "Guitar Player Magazine."

Although these arrangements have been written primarily for their entertainment content, you may find them useful for their etude value as well. I've listed below a number of solo guitar concepts and techniques along with the song titles in this folio that best illustrate their application.

Concepts/Techniques	Songs
Walking bass lines	"In A Mellow Tone"
	"Take The 'A' Train"
Big band, small group	"Don't Get Around Much Anymore"
Keyboard concepts	"Do Nothin' Till You Hear From Me"
Quartal (fourth) harmony	"I Got Bad (And That Ain't Good)
Combining Harmonics with regular tones	"In A Sentimental Mood"
Voicings mixing open strings with fretted notes	"Sophisticated Lady"
"Ghost notes" and "comping"	
Implying fast tempos with a two feeling	"It Don't Mean A Thing
Percussive effects	(If It Ain't Got That Swing)"
Developing independence between melody, accompaniment and bass voice	"Satin Doll"
Latin and jazz syncopation	"Caravan"
Close voicings	"Mood Indigo"
Wide stretch voicings	
Quartal harmony	
Tremolo study	"Prelude To A Kiss"

The music of Edward Kennedy "Duke" Ellington with its timeless, unforgettable melodies and subtle, rich and sometimes unexpected harmonies, often written for a big band sound, translates easily and naturally to the solo guitar. I had a ball writing every one of these arrangements and I hope you're going to have a ball playing them.

Howard Morgen

4

IN A MELLOW TONE

By
DUKE ELLINGTON and MILT GABLER
Arranged by HOWARD MORGEN

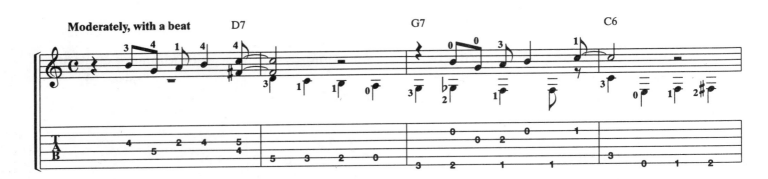

In A Mellow Tone - 2 - 1
TGF0036

DON'T GET AROUND MUCH ANYMORE

Words by
BOB RUSSEL
Music by
DUKE ELLINGTON
Arranged by HOWARD MORGEN

Don't Get Around Much Anymore - 2 - 2
TGF0036

DO NOTHIN' TILL YOU HEAR FROM ME

Words by
BOB RUSSELL
Music by
DUKE ELLINGTON
Arranged by HOWARD MORGEN

Do Nothin' Till You Hear From Me - 2 - 1
TGF0036

Do Nothin' Till You Hear From Me - 2 - 2
TGF0036

IN A SENTIMENTAL MOOD

By
DUKE ELLINGTON, IRVING MILLS
and **MANNY KURTZ**
Arranged by HOWARD MORGEN

TAKE THE A TRAIN

By
BILLY STRAYHORN and
THE DELTA RHYTHM BOYS
Arranged by HOWARD MORGEN

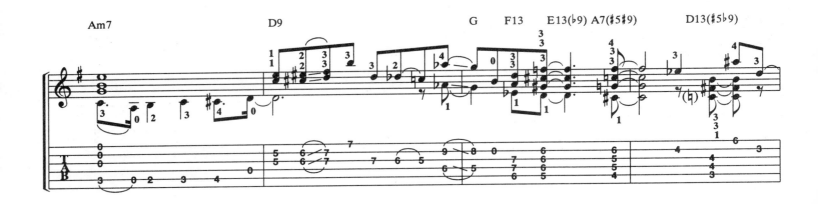

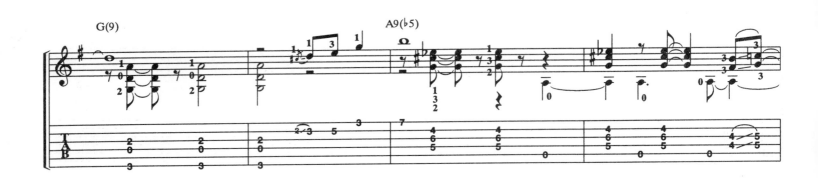

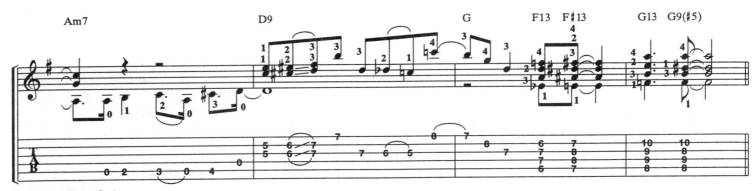

Take The A Train - 2 - 1
TGF0036

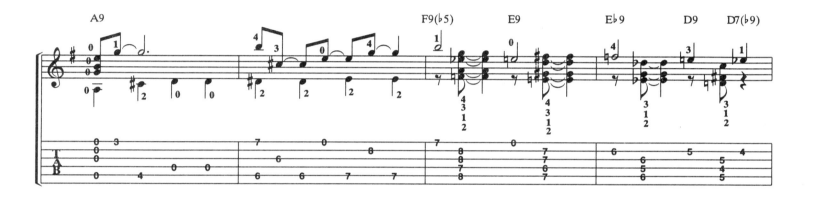

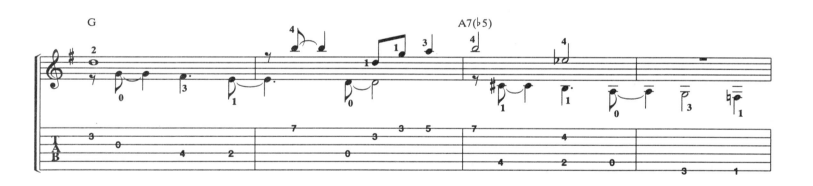

Take The A Train - 2 - 2
TGF0036

SOPHISTICATED LADY

Words by
IRVING MILLS and MITCHELL PARISH
Music by
DUKE ELLINGTON
Arranged by HOWARD MORGEN

Sophisticated Lady - 2 - 1
TGF0036

SATIN DOLL

Words and Music by
DUKE ELLINGTON, JOHNNY MERCER
and BILLY STRAYHORN
Arranged by HOWARD MORGEN

Satin Doll - 2 -1
TGF0036

MOOD INDIGO

By
DUKE ELLINGTON, IRVING MILLS
and **ALBANY BIGARD**
Arranged by HOWARD MORGEN

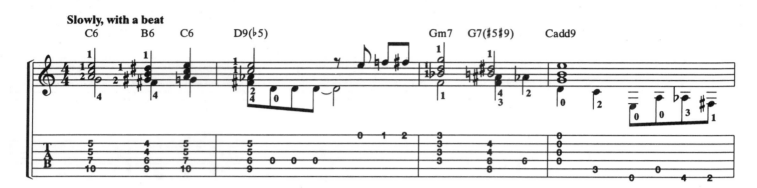

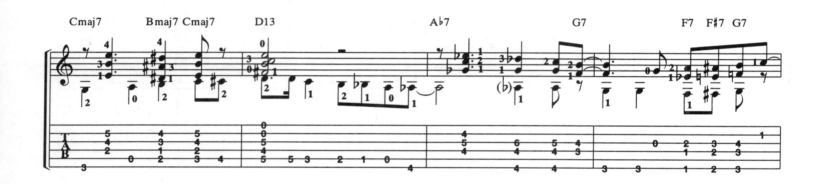

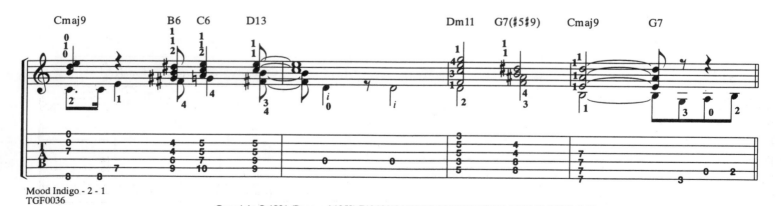

Mood Indigo - 2 - 1
TGF0036

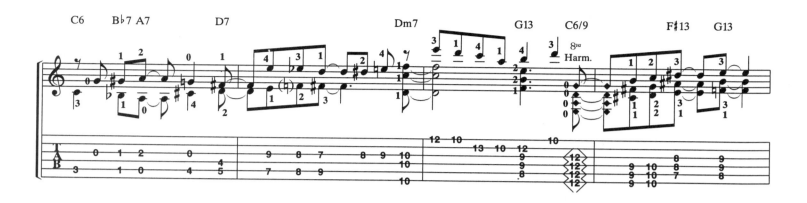

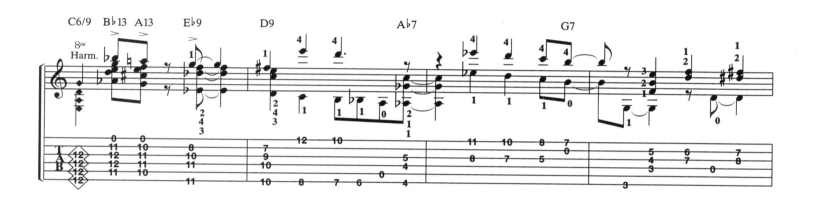

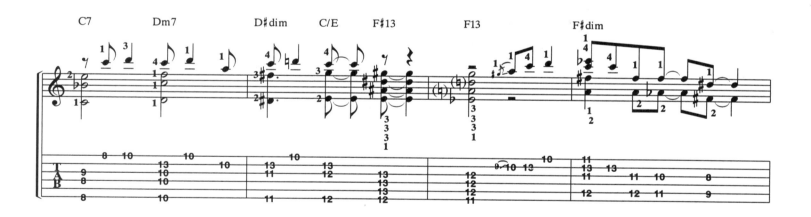

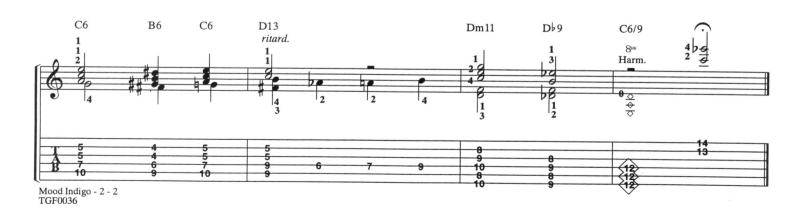

Mood Indigo - 2 - 2
TGF0036

IT DON'T MEAN A THING
(IF IT AIN'T GOT THAT SWING)

Words by
IRVING MILLS
Music by
DUKE ELLINGTON
Arranged by HOWARD MORGEN

It Don't Mean A Thing - 2 - 1
TGF0036

I GOT IT BAD AND THAT AIN'T GOOD

Words by
PAUL FRANCIS WEBSTER
Music by
DUKE ELLINGTON
Arranged by HOWARD MORGEN

I Got It Bad And That Ain't Good - 2 - 1
TGF0036

I Got It Bad And That Ain't Good - 2 - 2
TGF0036

CARAVAN

By
DUKE ELLINGTON, IRVING MILLS
and JUAN TIZOL
Arranged by HOWARD MORGEN

Caravan - 4 - 1
TGF0036

Caravan - 4 - 2
TGF0036

Caravan - 4 - 4
TGF0036

PRELUDE TO A KISS

By
DUKE ELLINGTON, IRVING MILLS
and IRVING GORDON
Arranged by HOWARD MORGEN

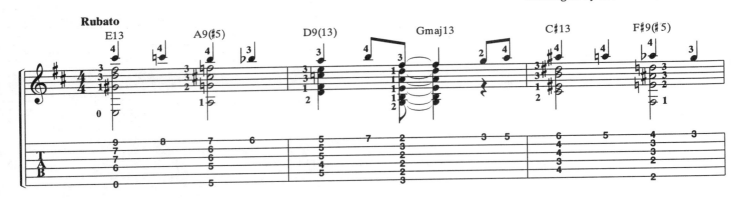

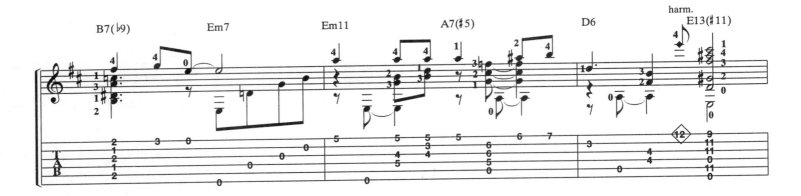

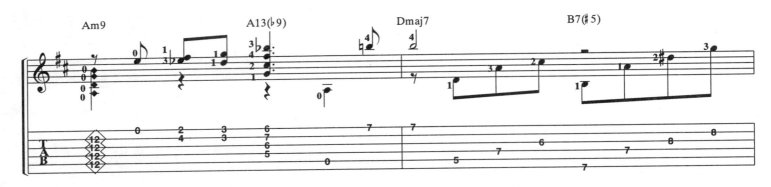

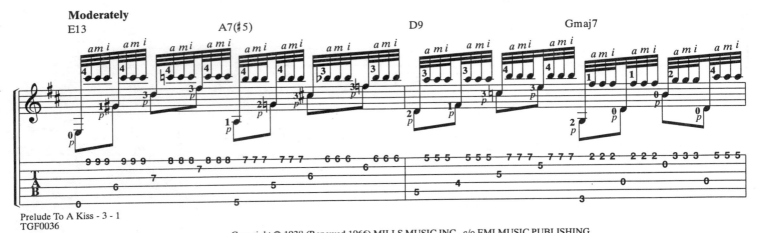

Prelude To A Kiss - 3 - 1
TGF0036

30

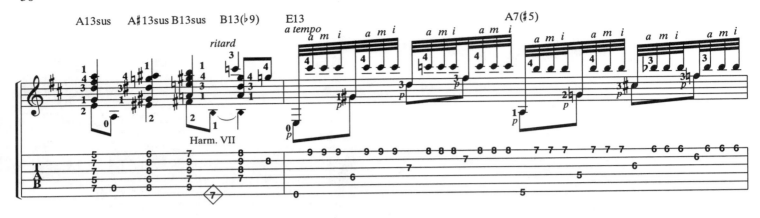

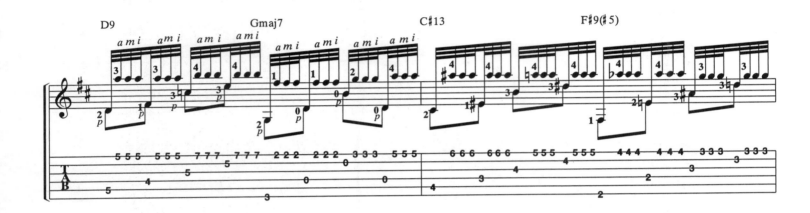

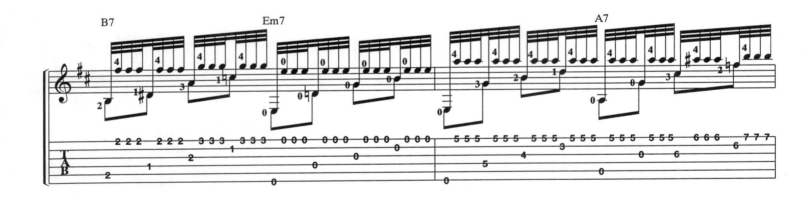

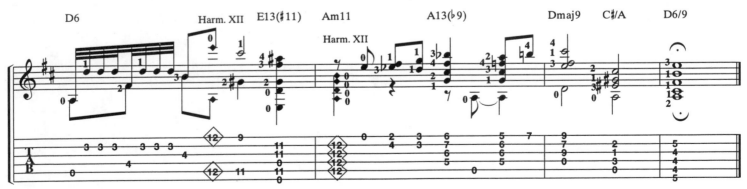

Prelude To A Kiss - 3 - 3
TGF0036

About the Author

Howard Morgen is an extraordinary guitarist dedicated to expanding the art of solo guitar. He is a columnist for Guitar Player magazine and the author of many books including: "Preparations," "Concepts," "Fingerstyle Favorites," "10 From Guitar Player," (all available from CPP/Belwin Inc.), and "Fingerstyle Jazz Images For Christmas" (available from Mel Bay, Inc.).

A former faculty member at the Manhattan School of Music, Mr. Morgen is currently teaching at the Guitar Study Center at The New School in New York. He is also very active performing concerts and conducting clinics throughout Europe and the U.S.

Aaron Stang
Editor/Fretted Instruments
CPP/Belwin, Inc.

Howard Morgen

Howard Morgen is an extraordinary guitarist dedicated to expanding the art of solo guitar. He is a columnist for *Guitar Player* magazine and the author of many books. A former faculty member at the Manhattan School of Music, Howard is currently teaching at the Guitar Study Center at The New School in New York. He is also very active performing concerts and conducting clinics throughout Europe and the U.S.

The Howard Morgen

Fingerstyle Jazz Series

10 from Guitar Player ®
____ (F3216GTX)

Solo guitar techniques such as contrapuntal motion, "harp" harmonics, substitution and embellishment. With ten complete arrangements, including: Angela (Theme from Taxi) • Misty • Tico Tico • Stella by Starlight • Theme from "Cheers" • It Might Be You • Those Were the Days • Moon River • Santa Claus Is Coming to Town.

Concepts: Arranging for Fingerstyle Guitar
____ (TPF0088)

Beginning with an explanation of how a bass line defines the harmonic scheme, this edition leads the player through dozens of fingerstyle arrangements. Including: Laura • Green Dolphin Street • The Shadow of Your Smile • Stompin' at the Savoy • Just Friends • Don't Blame Me • Nobody Does It Better.

Fingerstyle Favorites for the Fingerstyle Guitarist
____ (TPF0152)

Thirty-five wonderful arrangements for solo and duet. Includes: Vincent • Over the Rainbow • Georgia • You Are So Beautiful • Emily • Theme from *Ice Castles* (Through the Eyes of Love) • Invitation • You Are the Sunshine of My Life • Sittin' on the Dock of the Bay. Intermediate to advanced level.

Preparations: An Introduction to Fingerstyle Playing
____ (TPF0087)

An excellent introduction to the art of solo guitar playing. Useful to anyone who wants to become familiar with the techniques and concepts of fingerstyle solo guitar while learning the rudiments of music, notation, basic theory and the guitar fingerboard.

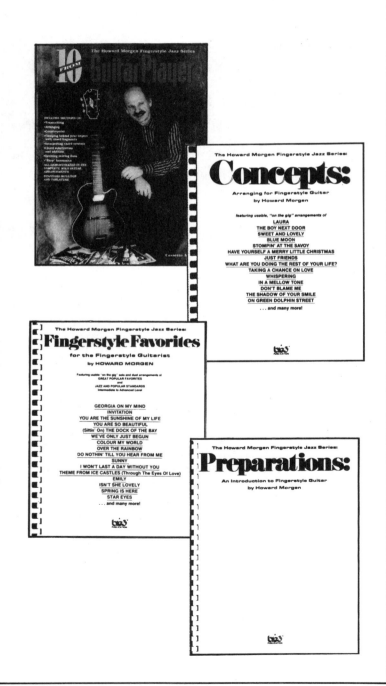